# YOUR KNOWLEDGE HAS VALUE

AF141542

- We will publish your bachelor's and master's thesis, essays and papers

- Your own eBook and book - sold worldwide in all relevant shops

- Earn money with each sale

Upload your text at www.GRIN.com
and publish for free

**Bibliographic information published by the German National Library:**

The German National Library lists this publication in the National Bibliography;
detailed bibliographic data are available on the Internet at http://dnb.dnb.de .

**Imprint:**

Copyright © 2016 GRIN Verlag, Open Publishing GmbH
Print and binding: Books on Demand GmbH, Norderstedt Germany
ISBN: 9783668420441

**This book at GRIN:**

http://www.grin.com/en/e-book/355921/student-recruitment-and-retention-in-
higher-education

**Mary Fiagbe**

# Student recruitment and retention in higher education

GRIN Publishing

**GRIN - Your knowledge has value**

Since its foundation in 1998, GRIN has specialized in publishing academic texts by students, college teachers and other academics as e-book and printed book. The website www.grin.com is an ideal platform for presenting term papers, final papers, scientific essays, dissertations and specialist books.

**Visit us on the internet:**

http://www.grin.com/

http://www.facebook.com/grincom

http://www.twitter.com/grin_com

**STUDENT RECRUITMENT AND RETENTION IN HIGHER EDUCATION**

Annotated Bibliography


UNIVERSITY OF WINDSOR

MENTORSHIP AND LEARNING

*Annotated Bibliography: Recruitment in Higher Education*

This bibliography uses six peer-reviewed journals to examine various strategies adopted by higher education institutions to promote the recruitment and retention of students. It also analyzes both positive and negative factors that may influence such strategies.

**Little, Michael W., Dennis O'Toole, and James Wetzel. 1997. "The Price Differential's Impact on Retention, Recruitment, and Quality in a Public University."** *Journal of Marketing for Higher Education* **8 (2): 37-51. DOI: 10.1300/J050v08n02_04. http://resolver.scholarsportal.info/resolve/08841241/v08i0002/37_tpdioraqiapu.**

This paper explores price differential marketing strategy as a way of attracting students to promote recruitment and retention in higher education institutions. It also makes note of the reasons why such a strategy is not used by institutions, and also how the strategy may prove to be efficient if properly communicated to the public (especially students). The article makes reference to the impact of tuition costs on student admissions and retention as well its relations to quality education. It therefore seeks to explain student recruitment and retention from a business point of view.

The article is useful because it takes into consideration how the perceived future benefits of higher education by students affect their enrolment and retention in these institutions. Meaning, students rely on the advantages and disadvantages of higher education –including salaries, importance and availability of jobs and future status –to determine their interest or willingness to enroll and remain in such institutions irrespective of the cost. The use of the price differential strategy also serves as a way to increase the resource flexibility of the institutions, give a perception of increased quality –business-wise, it refers to a price and quality relationship that promote brand positioning –and improve accountability.[1] On the other hand, in the case where students are not impressed with the future benefits, the high tuition cost becomes another reason affecting recruitment and retention. There is also the problem of implementing such strategies as well as the reluctance of other institutions (competition) to adopt such strategies.

---

[1] Little, Michael W., Dennis O'Toole, and James Wetzel. 1997. "The Price Differential's Impact on Retention, Recruitment, and Quality in a Public University." *Journal of Marketing for Higher Education* 8 (2): p40-41.

The article makes use of research findings to talk about other factors affecting recruitment and retention of students in higher education aside from this business related strategy. It states that demographic factors, family background and income, student perceptions and expectations, location, and reputation affect student enrolment and attrition levels. Thus, it covers a broad range of factors that affect recruitment and retention although it does not give any further explanations of such factors. The authors also concurred with the need for more research since the study was limited to currently enrolled students and did not include prospective ones.[2]

The authors were able to effectively examine the issue of price differential marketing strategy in respect to student recruitment and retention in higher education, while also acknowledging the fact that it served a beneficial purpose for higher education institutions not just students.

**Dumas-Hines, Frances A., Lessie L. Cochran, and Ellen U. Williams. "Promoting diversity: recommendations for recruitment and retention of minorities in higher education".** *College Student Journal* **35, no.3 (2001): 433+.** *Academic OneFile* **(accessed October 12, 2016).**
**http://go.galegroup.com.ezproxy.uwindsor.ca/ps/i.do?&id=GALE|A80744656&v=2.1&u=wind05901&it=r&p=AONE&sw=w**

This article provides recommendations on how to recruit and retain students in higher learning institutions to promote diversity through the use of literature reviews and research. It describes a number of both recruitment and retention methods including, the provision of financial incentives (such as scholarships and grants), outreach programs, and university marketing to encourage more student enrolment in postsecondary institutions. The journal also makes mention of academic mentoring, cultural diversity training, and self-esteem image activities. These act as strategies that aid in retention and help prevent self-isolation –one of the causes of low student retention.

The journal is relevant; it states various reasons responsible for low recruitment and retention of students in higher education institutions. It also helps institutions think about

---

[2] Little, O'Toole, and Wetzel, *Journal of Marketing for Higher Education* 8 (2): p50.

ways to promote entry and retention through the use of some of the mentioned activities and methods.

Although the article does state very important points in relation to how to promote diversity in the university through recruitment and retention methods, it however fails to point out that reduced admissions into these institutions are not limited to these problems. This is because other issues such as problems in the student selection process may cause restrictions to student recruitment and retention. It also just mainly talks about academic mentoring as a way to retain students, neglecting other means of encouraging retention. The article makes mention of university marketing as a way of recruitment but does not explain what it entails.

All things considered, the article is important and does state valid points in regard to higher education recruitments and retention strategies and their effects.

**Wang, A., Espinosa C., Long C., and Patel A. (2005). Team leaders and the honors freshman-year experience (1).** *Honors in Practice 1,* **129+. http://go.galegroup.com.ezproxy.uwindsor.ca/ps/i.do?&id=GALE|A165362539&v=2.1 &u=wind05901&it=r&p=AONE&sw=w&authCount=1#**

This article explains the need for both academic and social integration in preventing student attrition. It relies on statistical data that suggests that student attrition is more profound in the first year (freshman year) in order to establish a strategy to improve on student retention in higher education. The authors also make mention of how student isolation and social alienation account for less student engagement in both academic and campus activities. In regards to a workable solution, they introduce a program known as the Team Leader program –this includes the selection of students to serve as mentors, guides, role models, and resources to incoming students.

The journal is significant because it states the fact that in order to successful transition from high school to a higher education institution there is the need for both social and academic integration of the student. This promotes student persistence, hence lowering attrition levels. In doing this, it talks about a team leader program that uses current students of good academic standing to help new students. The article also shows the importance of experience in mentoring, as students chosen for the role have also been in a similar situation –

had mentors. This makes it easier for them to connect and interact efficiently with new students. In addition, the authors also mention how the team leaders (mentors) are trained to make them ready for their roles. This is a very important point because it points to the fact that the mentors are also learners and that in order for them to do a good job, they need to be trained and know what their roles and responsibilities are.

A notable strength in the article is that team leaders are not just involved with helping new students academically, but they also aid in the social aspects of the students lives. For instance, team leaders plan and organize social activities, symposiums, and go on field trips with their team members. These activities not only help in building students' skills but also encourage the development of social relationships between the leader and the students, as well as the members of the team. This social relationship helps to bond students together, making both social and academic integration easier. Not only is it important to develop a good relationship among students, there is a need for a good and healthy relationship between students and professors –which is one of the purposes of the team leader program (the facilitating of a good relationship between students and professors). As such, the team leaders play a vital role in every aspect of a new student's university life, while also honing their leadership skills.

Even with these advantages, the article only places emphasis on how fellow students can contribute to the development and retention of new students. It fails to elaborate on the role of faculty staff, especially professors to the growth and retention of students. I make reference to this because, in order to make students feel welcome and hence encourage retention, the role of higher education institution staff is also very important. For instance, even the team leaders who apply for the positions would not do so or may even have dropped out if they did not feel supported or have confidence in their professors.

This article does serve its purpose in its analysis of how to enhance the first year experiences of new students through the use of fellow students as mentors and guides, in order to reduce dropout rates and retain students. It also considers the benefits such an opportunity gives the team leaders –fulfillment, leadership skills, and experience –and not just freshman students.

Elliott, Kevin M. and Margaret A. Healy. 2001. "Key Factors Influencing Student Satisfaction Related to Recruitment and Retention." *Journal of Marketing for Higher Education* 10 (4): 1-11. DOI: 10.1300/J050v10n04_01. http://resolver.scholarsportal.info/resolve/08841241/v10i0004/1_kfissrtrar.

This article examines how student satisfaction derived from educational experience contributes to recruitment and retention of students in higher education. It also focuses on how recruitment strategies may be dependent on analyzing different aspects of 'students' educational experiences'.[3] This study-based research article, in relation to student recruitment and retention, uses student importance, satisfaction, and performance gaps as a way to determine overall student educational experience.

To increase recruitment, the article focuses on the need to identify what students consider as being important to them so as to gain their attention. To encourage retention, students have to be satisfied with their educational experiences –through the provision of quality education. Performance gaps also play an important role in student retention. They help determine how motivated students will be in order to get them to remain in higher education institutions. In a situation where performance gaps are wide or where there is low performance, students may be discouraged from staying in school. A vice versa situation promotes competition, which helps to keep students in higher education. The authors also noted that every student would have different aspects of their educational experiences that they value as very important to their overall student satisfaction. Thus, helping to determining whether or not they will be interested in enrolling and staying in these institutions.

Importance is placed on the interrelation of both student recruitment and retention since one cannot do with the other. This is because, in order to promote recruitment, there is the need for current students to feel satisfied as they serve as a mode of promotion of higher education institutions (students who stay in school, promote their schools to prospective students). It states the limitations of the study in respect to the factors that influence student recruitment and retention. This includes the fact that it fails to examine other relevant areas that affect recruitment and retention, for example, the reputation of the institution as well as the costs associated with higher education. Although it makes mention of performance gaps, it

---

[3] Elliott, Kevin M. and Margaret A. Healy. 2001. "Key Factors Influencing Student Satisfaction Related to Recruitment and Retention." *Journal of Marketing for Higher Education* 10 (4): p1.

does not elaborate on what exactly it entails – an example being how student academic performance or grades as well as student competition impact attrition levels.

Consequently, the article states very important factors that influence student recruitment and retention through the use of a study. On the other hand, due to the fact that it only considers current student and not prospective ones, it requires more research since current students may have different perspectives from those who are yet to gain admission into higher education institutions.

**Walker, L. S. (1999). Bridging the Gap: Students' Role in Recruitment and Retention.** *Guidance & Counseling*, **15(1), 13.** http://search.ebscohost.com.ezproxy.uwindsor.ca/login.aspx?direct=true&db=a9h&AN=7267699&site=ehost-live

This paper examines the contribution of first year students (student ambassadors), who act as "caring connectors" in helping to facilitate prospective students' transition into higher education institutions. It uses a three-stage model –inviting, involving, and integrating –as a way of promoting student recruitment and retention. The author also describes the importance of student partnerships and places value on the need for student ambassadors to be caring, connected, and committed, when it comes to recruitment and retention practices.

The article is relevant because it recognizes that for prospective students to feel comfortable and interested in gaining admission and staying in school, they need to feel invited and have confidence in the environment. It also makes mention of the use of a student ambassador program to develop and refine the academic skills of incoming students in order to create a community of academically competent students so they can adapt to university life. The use of the three-stage model helps students learn important strategies to help them feel more included, involved, and valued in higher education institutions. Some of the activities involved in the model include school visits, talks, and the use of informational materials such as videos to inform or educate incoming students of how to cope or what they need to know about such institutions.

Although the article states that the program helps new students to establish a sense of belonging, it however fails explain how social integration plays a huge part in student recruitment and retention. It just highlights social skills as one of the three essential elements of student integration found in research findings. As such, the program should not only focus on helping students academically, but should also help them in the social aspect of their university lives. One important point noted in the paper is the need for student ambassadors to be effectively trained in order for them to perform their duties efficiently as connectors and helpers of prospective students. The author also mentions the use of conversational sessions to with help student integration, which in turn promotes retention.

Conclusively, the paper demonstrates how important first-year students are in helping to promote student recruitment, while reducing attrition. This is partly due to the fact that such students are able to better understand and communicate with prospective students since they were in the same category not long ago.

**Goralski, Margaret A., and Ahmad Tootoonchi. "Recruitment of International Students to the United States: Implications for institutions of higher education".** *International Journal of Education Research* **10, no.1 (2015): 53+.** *Academic OneFile* **(accessed October 16, 2016).**
**http://go.galegroup.com.ezproxy.uwindsor.ca/ps/i.do?&id=GALE|A417473393&v=2.1 &u=wind05901&it=r&p=AONE&sw=w&authCount=1#**

This research paper evaluates the recruitment of international students into higher education institutions, the domestic and global factors affecting such recruitments, and the impact of technology (distance learning program) in student recruitment and retention. The rise of international students in institutions of higher education has prompted the need for more strategies in recruiting and retaining them.

In regards to how relevant the paper is, the authors have pointed out certain important facts. They describe how the state can play a role in the recruitment of students –example being the reputation of a country's academic system. This shows that it is not just the institutions that can put in efforts to encourage recruitment and retention. Instead, the way students view a particular country may serve as a factor for recruitment and low attrition levels. The research study also states various factors affecting student recruitment (reasons why students may enroll in certain institutions). This includes, enhancing career opportunities, gaining experience for future jobs, the reputation and the academic quality of the institution, as well as information received from the Internet, social media, or other students. The journal recognizes that online learning (distance education) also poses a threat to student recruitment and retention in higher education institutions.

The journal takes note of the fact that the recruitment of international students is competitive. However, it does not elaborate on the fact the recruitment of just the best students by some institutions or of any student regardless of their academic proficiency, affects recruitment and attrition levels. This is because, when such institutions seek out only the best students or vice versa, the enrollment and retention of other students are affected. Some students may not feel qualified enough to enroll in certain higher education institutions while some may feel overqualified. On the other hand, the paper also acknowledges recruitment trips as one of the way to encourage student recruitment. This is done in order to gain international recognition, promote higher education institutions, and form partnerships between institutions.

The paper's examination of international student recruitment and retention in higher education institutions not only focuses on the factors affecting such issues. It also explains the advantages and problems caused by such recruitments in the home countries of international students.

# YOUR KNOWLEDGE HAS VALUE